66 Teachings of Jesus for KIDS to Memorize

Matthew 10:16

READ IT →

"Behold, I send you out as sheep among wolves. Therefore be wise as serpents and harmless as doves."

FILL IN THE BLANKS: →

"_____, I send you out as _____ among _____. Therefore be _____ as serpents and _____ as _____."

COLOR →

Therefore be wise as serpents and harmless as doves.

Matthew 5:

Give to him who asks turn away him who de from yo

FILL IN THE BLANKS: →

"_____ to him wh away h

COLOR →

How to Use this Book:

READ IT:
Read the verse, fill in the blanks, then color!

FILL IN THE BLANKS:
_____ the verse, fill in the _____, then color!

COLOR:

Read the verse, fill in the blanks, then color!

On the back of each page, write the verse from memory!

READ IT: ➡

"Follow me, and I will make you fishers of men."

FILL IN THE BLANKS: ➡

" _____ me, and I will ____ you _____ of ___."

COLOR: ➡

Follow me, and I will make you fishers of men.

WRITE IT ➡

Matthew 5:2

READ IT: ➡

"Blessed are the poor in spirit: for theirs is the kingdom of heaven."

FILL IN THE ➡
BLANKS:

"_____ are the _____ in _____: for theirs is the _____ of _____."

COLOR: ➡

Blessed are the poor in spirit: for theirs is the kingdom of heaven.

WRITE IT ➡

Matthew 5:4

READ IT: ➡

"Blessed are they that mourn:
for they shall be comforted."

FILL IN THE BLANKS: ➡

"_____ are they that _____:

For ____ shall be _____."

COLOR: ➡

Blessed are
they that
mourn: for
they shall be
comforted.

WRITE IT ➡

Matthew 5:11

READ IT: ➡

"Blessed are you, when men shall revile you, and persecute you, and shall say all manner of evil against you falsely, for my sake."

FILL IN THE BLANKS: ➡

"_____ are you, when ___ shall _____ you, and _____ you, and shall ___ all manner of ____ against you _____, for my ____."

COLOR: ➡

Blessed are you, when men shall revile you, and persecute you.

WRITE IT ➡

Matthew 5:13

READ IT: ➡

"You are the salt of the earth: but if the salt has lost its flavor, with what will it be salted?"

FILL IN THE BLANKS: ➡

"____ are the ____ of the _____: but if the ____ has ____ its _____, with what ____ it be _____?"

COLOR: ➡

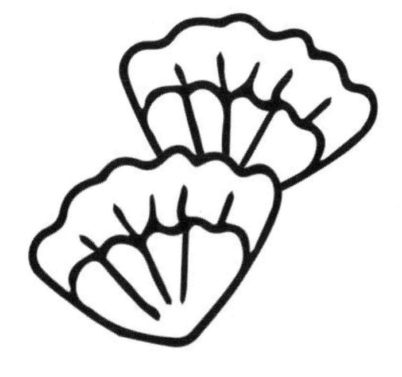

You are the salt of the earth.

WRITE IT ➡

Matthew 5:14

READ IT: ➡

"You are the light of the world. A city located on a hill can't be hidden."

FILL IN THE BLANKS: ➡

"_ _ _ are the _ _ _ _ _ of the _ _ _ _ _. A _ _ _ _ located on a _ _ _ _ can't be _ _ _ _ _ _."

COLOR: ➡

You are the light of the world. A city located on a hill can't be hidden.

WRITE IT ➡

Matthew 5:16

"Even so, let your light shine before men, that they may see your good works and glorify your Father who is in heaven."

FILL IN THE BLANKS: ➡

"Even so, let your _ _ _ _ _ shine _ _ _ _ _ _ _ men, that they _ _ _ see your _ _ _ _ works and _ _ _ _ _ _ _ your _ _ _ _ _ _ who is in _ _ _ _ _ _ ."

COLOR: ➡

Even so, let your light shine before men.

WRITE IT ➡

Matthew 5:17

READ IT: ➡

"Don't think that I came to destroy the law or the prophets. I didn't come to destroy but to fulfill."

FILL IN THE BLANKS: ➡

"Don't _____ that I ____ to _____ the law or the _____. I didn't ____ to destroy but to _____."

COLOR: ➡

I didn't come to destroy but to fulfill.

WRITE IT ➡

Matthew 5:37

READ IT: ➡

"But let your 'Yes' be 'Yes' and your 'No' be 'No.' Whatever is more than these is of the evil one."

FILL IN THE BLANKS: ➡

But ___ your '___' be 'Yes' and ____ 'No' be '__.' _____ is ____ than these is of the ____ one.

COLOR: ➡

But let your 'Yes' be 'Yes' and your 'No' be 'No'.

WRITE IT ➡

Matthew 5:42

READ IT: ➡

"Give to him who asks you, and don't turn away him who desires to borrow from you."

FILL IN THE BLANKS: ➡

"_ _ _ _ to him who _ _ _ _ you, and don't _ _ _ _ away him who _ _ _ _ _ _ _ to _ _ _ _ _ _ from you."

COLOR: ➡

Give to him who asks you.

WRITE IT ➡

Matthew 5:44

READ IT: ➡

"But I tell you, love your enemies, bless those who curse you, do good to those who hate you, and pray for those who mistreat you and persecute you."

FILL IN THE BLANKS: ➡

But I _____ you, love your _____, bless those who _____ you, do _____ to those who _____ you, and _____ for those who _____ you and persecute you.

COLOR: ➡

Love your enemies, bless those who curse you.

WRITE IT ➡

Matthew 6:3-4

READ IT: ➡

"But when you do merciful deeds, don't let your left hand know what your right hand does, so that your merciful deeds may be in secret."

FILL IN THE ➡
BLANKS:

"But when you do _____ deeds, don't let your ____ hand know what your _____ hand ____, so that your merciful _____ may be in _____."

COLOR: ➡

Don't let your left hand know what your right hand does.

WRITE IT ➡

Matthew 6:6

READ IT: ➡

"When you pray, enter into your inner room, and having shut your door, pray to your Father who is in secret; and your Father who sees in secret will

FILL IN THE BLANKS: ➡ reward you openly."

When you _____, enter into your _____ room, and having _____ your door, pray to your _____ who is in _____; and your Father who _____ in secret will _____ you openly.

COLOR: ➡

Your Father who is in secret will reward you openly.

WRITE IT ➡

Matthew 6:25

READ IT: ➡

"Therefore I tell you, don't be anxious for your life: what you will eat, or what you will drink; nor yet for your body, what you will wear."

FILL IN THE BLANKS: ➡

"Therefore I _ _ _ _ you, don't be _ _ _ _ _ _ _ for your _ _ _ _: what you will _ _ _, or what you will _ _ _ _ _; nor yet for your _ _ _ _, what you will _ _ _ _."

COLOR: ➡

Don't be anxious for your life.

WRITE IT ➡

Matthew 6:33

READ IT: ➡

"But seek first God's Kingdom and his righteousness; and all these things will be given to you as well."

FILL IN THE ➡
BLANKS:

"But _____ first God's _____ and his _____; and all these _____ will be _____ to you as well."

COLOR: ➡

But seek first
God's Kingdom
and his
righteousness.

WRITE IT ➡

WRITE IT ➡

Matthew 7:7

READ IT: ➡

"Ask, and it will be given you. Seek, and you will find. Knock, and it will be opened for you."

FILL IN THE BLANKS: ➡

"___, and it will be _____ you. ____, and you will ____. _____, and it will be _____ for you."

COLOR: ➡

Seek, and you will find.

Matthew 7 13

READ IT: ➡

"Enter in by the narrow gate; for the gate is wide and the way is broad that leads to destruction, and there are many who enter in by it."

FILL IN THE BLANKS: ➡

"_____ in by the _____ gate; for the _____ is wide and the way is _____ that leads to _____, and there are _____ who enter in by it."

COLOR: ➡

Enter in by the narrow gate.

WRITE IT ➡

Matthew 7:24

READ IT: ➡

"Everyone therefore who hears these words of mine and does them, I will liken him to a wise man who built his house on a rock."

FILL IN THE BLANKS: ➡

"Everyone therefore who _____ these _____ of mine and does them, I will _____ him to a wise ___ who built his _____ on a ____."

COLOR: ➡

I will liken him to a wise man who built his house on a rock.

WRITE IT ➡

WRITE IT ➡

Mathew 9:13

READ IT: ➡

"But you go and learn what this means: 'I desire mercy, and not sacrifice,' for I came not to call the righteous, but sinners to repentance."

FILL IN THE BLANKS: ➡

"But you go and _____ what this means: 'I _____ mercy, and not _____,' for I came not to _____ the righteous, but _____ to repentance."

COLOR: ➡

But you go and learn what this means: 'I desire mercy, and not sacrifice'.

WRITE IT ➡

Matthew 9:37

READ IT: ➡

"The harvest indeed is plentiful, but the laborers are few. Pray therefore that the Lord of the harvest will send out laborers into his harvest."

FILL IN THE BLANKS: ➡

"The _____ indeed is _____, but the _____ are few. Pray therefore that the ____ of the harvest will ____ out laborers ____ his harvest."

COLOR: ➡

The harvest indeed is plentiful, but the laborers are few.

WRITE IT ➡

Matthew 10:16

READ IT: ➡

"Behold, I send you out as sheep among wolves. Therefore be wise as serpents and harmless as doves."

FILL IN THE BLANKS: ➡

"_____, I send you out as _____ among _____. Therefore be ____ as serpents and _____ as _____."

COLOR: ➡

Therefore be wise as serpents and harmless as doves.

WRITE IT ➡

Matthew 10:27

"What I tell you in the darkness, speak in the light; and what you hear whispered in the ear, proclaim on the housetops."

FILL IN THE BLANKS: ➡

"What I ____ you in the _____, speak in the _____; and what you ____ whispered in the ___, proclaim on the _____."

COLOR: ➡

What I tell you in the darkness, speak in the light.

WRITE IT ➡

Matthew 10:28

READ IT: ➡

"Don't be afraid of those who kill the body, but are not able to kill the soul. Rather, fear him who is able to destroy both soul and body in Hell."

FILL IN THE BLANKS: ➡

"Don't be _____ of those who ____ the ____, but are not able to kill the ____. Rather, ____ him who is able to _____ both soul and ____ in Hell."

COLOR: ➡

Don't be afraid of those who kill the body, but are not able to kill the soul.

WRITE IT ➡

Matthew 10:29-31

READ IT: ➡

"Aren't two sparrows sold for a penny? Not one of them falls to the ground apart from your Father's will. But the very hairs of your head are all numbered."

FILL IN THE BLANKS: ➡

"Aren't two _____ sold for a _____? Not one of them _____ to the _____ apart from your Father's _____. But the very _____ of your ____ are all _____."

COLOR: ➡

But the very hairs on your head are all numbered.

WRITE IT ➡

Matthew 10:39

READ IT: ➡

"He who seeks his life will lose it; and he who loses his life for my sake will find it."

FILL IN THE BLANKS: ➡

"He who _____ his ____ will lose it; and he who _____ his life for my ____ will ____ it."

COLOR: ➡

He who loses his life for my sake will find it.

WRITE IT ➡

Matthew 11:28

READ IT: ➡

"Come to me, all you who labor
and are heavily burdened,
and I will give you rest."

FILL IN THE BLANKS: ➡

"_____ to me, all you who _____
and are _____ burdened,
and I will _____ you _____."

COLOR: ➡

I will give
you rest.

WRITE IT ➡

Matthew 11:29

READ IT: ➡

"Take my yoke upon you and learn from me, for I am gentle and humble in heart; and you will find rest for your souls."

FILL IN THE BLANKS: ➡

"Take my ____ upon you and _____ from me, for I am _____ and _____ in heart; and you will find ____ for your _____."

COLOR: ➡

I am gentle and humble in heart.

WRITE IT ➡

Matthew 12:35

READ IT: ➡

"The good man out of his good treasure brings out good things, and the evil man out of his evil treasure brings out evil things."

FILL IN THE BLANKS: ➡

"The ____ man out of his good _____ bring out good _____, and the evil ___ out of his ____ treasure _____ out evil _____."

COLOR: ➡

The good man out of his good treasure brings out good things.

WRITE IT ➡

Matthew 12:50

READ IT: ➡

"For whoever does the will of my Father who is in heaven, he is my brother, and sister, and mother."

FILL IN THE BLANKS: ➡

"For _____ does the ____ of my _____ who is in _____, he is my _____, and sister, and _____."

COLOR: ➡

He is my brother, and sister, and mother.

WRITE IT ➡

WRITE IT ➡

Matthew 13:44

READ IT: ➡

"The Kingdom of Heaven is like treasure hidden in the field, which a man found and hid. In his joy, he goes and sells all that he has and buys that field."

FILL IN THE BLANKS: ➡

"The _____ of Heaven is like _____ hidden in the _____, which a ___ found and ___. In his ___, he goes and _____ all that he has and _____ that field."

COLOR: ➡

In his joy, he goes and sells all that he has and buys that field.

Matthew 13:45

"The Kingdom of Heaven is like a man who is a merchant seeking fine pearls, who having found one pearl of great price, he went and sold all that he had

FILL IN THE BLANKS: ➡ and bought it."

"The Kingdom of _____ is like a ___ who is a merchant seeking ____ pearls, who _____ found one _____ of great _____, he went and ____ all that he had and _____ it."

COLOR: ➡

He went and sold all that he had and bought it.

WRITE IT ➡

WRITE IT ➡

Matthew 15:10-11

READ IT: ➡

"Hear, and understand. That which enters into the mouth doesn't defile the man; but that which proceeds out of the mouth, this defiles the man."

FILL IN THE BLANKS: ➡

"_____, and _____. That which _____ into the _____ doesn't defile the man; but that which _____ out of the mouth, that _____ the man."

COLOR: ➡

That which proceeds out of the mouth, this defiles the man.

WRITE IT ➡

Matthew 17:20

READ IT: ➡

"If you have faith as a grain of mustard seed, you will tell this mountain, 'Move from here to there,' and it will move; and nothing will be impossible for you."

FILL IN THE BLANKS: ➡

"If you have _____ as a _____ of _____ seed, you will tell this _____, 'Move from ____ to there,' and it will ____; and _____ will be _____ for you."

COLOR: ➡

Nothing will be impossible for you.

WRITE IT ➡

Matthew 18:3

READ IT: ➡

"Most certainly I tell you, unless you turn and become as little children, you will in no way enter into the Kingdom of Heaven."

FILL IN THE BLANKS: ➡

"Most _____ I tell you, _____ you turn and _____ as little _____, you will in no ___ enter into the _____ of Heaven."

COLOR: ➡

Turn and become as little children.

WRITE IT ➡

Matthew 18:10-11

READ IT: ➡

"See that you don't despise one of these little ones, for I tell you that in heaven their angels always see the face of my Father who is in heaven."

FILL IN THE BLANKS: ➡

"See to it that you don't _____ one of these _____ ones, for I ____ you that in _____ their _____ always see the ____ of my _____ who is in _____."

COLOR: ➡

See to it that you don't despise one of these little ones.

WRITE IT ➡

Matthew 18:12

READ IT: ➡

"If a man has one hundred sheep, and one of them goes astray, doesn't he leave the ninety-nine, go to the mountains, and seek that which has gone astray?"

FILL IN THE
BLANKS: ➡

"If a ___ has one _____ sheep, and ___ of them ____ astray, doesn't he _____ the ninety-nine, go to the _____, and seek that _____ has gone _____?"

COLOR: ➡

Doesn't he ...
seek that
which has
gone astray?

WRITE IT ➡

WRITE IT ➡

Matthew 18:19

READ IT: ➡

"Assuredly I tell you, that if two of you will agree on earth concerning anything that they will ask, it will be done for them by my Father who is in heaven."

FILL IN THE BLANKS: ➡

"_____ I tell you, that if ___ of you will _____ on earth concerning _____ that they will ___, it will be ____ for them by my _____ who is in _____."

COLOR: ➡

It will be done for them by my Father who is in heaven.

WRITE IT ➡

Matthew 18:20

READ IT: ➡

"For where two or three are gathered together in my name, there I am in the middle of them."

FILL IN THE BLANKS: ➡

"For _____ two or _____ are gathered _____ in my ____, there I am in the _____ of them."

COLOR: ➡

Where two or three are gathered together in my name, there I am.

WRITE IT ➡

WRITE IT ➡

Matthew 19:14

READ IT: ➡

"Allow the little children, and don't forbid them to come to me; for the Kingdom of Heaven belongs to ones like these."

FILL IN THE BLANKS: ➡

"_____ the little _____, and don't _____ them to ____ to me; for the _____ of Heaven belongs to ____ like _____."

COLOR: ➡

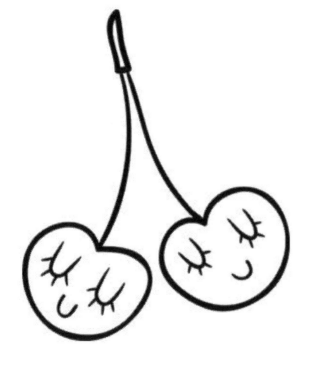

Allow the little children, and don't forbid them to come to me.

WRITE IT ➡

Matthew 19:24

READ IT: ➡

"I tell you, it is easier for a camel to go through a needle's eye than for a rich man to enter into God's Kingdom."

FILL IN THE BLANKS: ➡

"I _____ you, it is _____ for a camel to go _____ a needle's eye than for a _____ man to _____ into God's _____."

COLOR: ➡

It is easier for a camel to go through a needle's eye.

WRITE IT ➡

Matthew 19:30

READ IT: ➡

"But many will be last who are first, and first who are last."

FILL IN THE BLANKS: ➡

"But _____ will be _____ who are _____, and _____ who are _____."

COLOR: ➡

But many will be last who are first, and first who are last.

WRITE IT ➡

Matthew 20:27-28

READ IT: ➡

"Whoever desires to be first among you shall be your bondservant, even as the Son of Man came not to be served, but to serve.

FILL IN THE BLANKS: ➡

"Whoever _____ to be _____ among you shall be your bondservant, ____ as the ___ of Man came not to be _____, but to _____."

COLOR: ➡

The Son of Man came not to be served, but to serve.

WRITE IT ➡

WRITE IT ➡

Matthew 22:21

READ IT: ➡

"Give therefore to Caesar the things that are Caesar's, and to God the things that are God's."

FILL IN THE BLANKS: ➡

"Give _____ to _____ the _____ that are Caesar's, and to ___ the _____ that are God's."

COLOR: ➡

Give to God the things that are God's.

WRITE IT ➡

WRITE IT ➡

Matthew 23:11-12

READ IT: ➡

"But he who is greatest among you will be your servant. Whoever exalts himself will be humbled, and whoever humbles himself will be exalted."

FILL IN THE ➡
BLANKS:

"But he is who is _____ among you will be your _____. Whoever _____ himself will be _____, and whoever _____ himself will be _____."

COLOR: ➡

But he who is greatest among you will be your servant.

WRITE IT ➡

WRITE IT ➡

Matthew 24:4-5

READ IT: ➡

"Be careful that no one leads you astray. For many will come in my name, saying, 'I am the Christ,' and will lead many astray."

FILL IN THE BLANKS: ➡

"Be _____ that no one _____ you _____. For ____ will come in my ____, saying, 'I am the _____,' and will ____ many _____."

COLOR: ➡

Be careful that no one leads you astray.

WRITE IT ➡

WRITE IT ➡

Matthew 24:27

READ IT: ➡

"For as the lightning flashes from the east, and is seen even to the west, so will the coming of the Son of Man be."

FILL IN THE BLANKS: ➡

"For as the _____ flashes from the _____, and is ____ even to the ____, so will the _____ of the Son of ___ be."

COLOR: ➡

So will the coming of the Son of Man be.

WRITE IT ➡

Matthew 24:35

READ IT: ➡

"Heaven and earth will pass away, but my words will not pass away."

FILL IN THE BLANKS: ➡

"_____ and _____ will pass ____, but my _____ will not ____ away."

COLOR: ➡

Heaven and earth will pass away, but my words will not pass away.

WRITE IT ➡

WRITE IT ➡

Matthew 25:13

READ IT: ➡

"Watch therefore, for you don't know the day nor the hour in which the Son of Man is coming."

FILL IN THE BLANKS: ➡

"_____ therefore, for you don't ____ the ___ nor the ____ in which the ___ of Man is _____."

COLOR: ➡

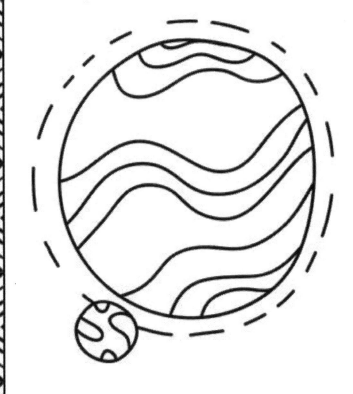

You don't know the day nor the hour.

WRITE IT ➡

WRITE IT ➡

Matthew 25:40

READ IT: ➡

"Most certainly I tell you, because you did it to one of the least of these my brothers, you did it to me.'"

FILL IN THE BLANKS: ➡

"____ certainly I ____ you, because you ___ it to one of the _____ of these my _____, you did it to __."

COLOR: ➡

Because you did it to one of the least of these my brothers, you did it to me.

WRITE IT ➡

WRITE IT ➡

Matthew 26:52

READ IT: ➡

"All those who take the sword will die by the sword."

FILL IN THE BLANKS: ➡

"All _____ who _____ the _____ will ____ by the sword."

COLOR: ➡

All those who take the sword will die by the sword.

WRITE IT ➡

WRITE IT ➡

Matthew 28:19

READ IT: ➡

"Go and make disciples of all nations, baptizing them in the name of the Father and of the Son and of the Holy Spirit."

FILL IN THE BLANKS: ➡

"Go and ____ disciples of all _____, baptizing them in the ____ of the _____ and of the ___ and of the ____ Spirit."

COLOR: ➡

Go and make disciples of all nations.

WRITE IT ➡

John 3:8

READ IT: ➡

"The wind blows where it wants to, and you hear its sound, but don't know where it comes from and where it is going. So is everyone who is born of the Spirit."

FILL IN THE BLANKS: ➡

"The _____ blows where it _____ to, and you ____ its _____, but don't know _____ it comes from or _____ it is _____. So is _____ who is ____ of the _____."

COLOR: ➡

So is everyone who is born of the Spirit.

WRITE IT ➡

John 3:14-15

READ IT: ➡

"As Moses lifted up the serpent in the wilderness, even so must the Son of Man be lifted up, that whoever believes in him should not perish, but have eternal life."

FILL IN THE ➡
BLANKS:

"As _____ lifted up the _____ in the _____, even so must the ____ of Man be _____ up, that whoever _____ in him should not _____, but have _____ life."

COLOR: ➡

Even so must the Son of Man be lifted up.

WRITE IT ➡

WRITE IT ➡

John 3:16

READ IT: ➡

"For God so loved the world, that he gave his one and only Son, that whoever believes in him should not perish, but have eternal life."

FILL IN THE BLANKS: ➡

"For God so _____ the world, that he ____ his one and ____ Son, that _____ believes in him should not _____, but have _____ life."

COLOR: ➡

Whoever believes in him should not perish, but have eternal life.

WRITE IT ➡

WRITE IT ➡

John 4:14

READ IT: ➡

"Whoever drinks of the water that I will give him will never thirst again."

FILL IN THE BLANKS: ➡

"_____ drinks of the _____ that I will ____ him will _____ thirst _____."

COLOR: ➡

Whoever drinks of the water that I will give him will never thirst again.

WRITE IT ➡

John 4:24

READ IT: ➡

"God is spirit, and those who worship him must worship in spirit and truth."

FILL IN THE BLANKS: ➡

"God is _____, and those who _____ him _____ worship in _____ and _____."

COLOR: ➡

Those who worship Him must worship in spirit and truth.

WRITE IT ➡

John 5:24

READ IT: ➡

"Most certainly I tell you, he who hears my word and believes him who sent me has eternal life, and doesn't come into judgment."

FILL IN THE BLANKS: ➡

"Most _____ I tell you, he who _____ my ____ and _____ him who sent me has _____ life, and doesn't come into _____."

COLOR: ➡

He who hears my word and believes him who sent me has eternal life.

WRITE IT ➡

WRITE IT ➡

John 6:51

READ IT: ➡

"I am the living bread which came down out of heaven. If anyone eats of this bread, he will live forever."

FILL IN THE BLANKS: ➡

"I am the _____ bread which _____ down out of _____. If _____ eats of this _____, he will _____ forever."

COLOR: ➡

I am the living bread which came down out of heaven.

WRITE IT →

WRITE IT →

John 7:37-38

READ IT: ➡

"If anyone is thirsty, let him come to me and drink! He who believes in me, as the Scripture has said, from within him will flow rivers of living water."

FILL IN THE BLANKS: ➡

"If anyone is _____, let him come to me and _____! He who _____ in me, as the _____ has said, from _____ him will flow _____ of living _____."

COLOR: ➡

If anyone is thirsty, Let him come to me and drink!

WRITE IT ➡

WRITE IT ➡

John 8:12

READ IT: ➡

"I am the light of the world. He who follows me will not walk in the darkness, but will have the light of life."

FILL IN THE BLANKS: ➡

"I am the _____ of the _____. He who _____ me will not ____ in the _____, but will have the _____ of ____."

COLOR: ➡

I am the Light of the world.

WRITE IT ➡

John 8:31-32

READ IT: ➡

"If you remain in my word, then you are truly my disciples. You will know the truth, and the truth will make you free."

FILL IN THE BLANKS: ➡

"If you _____ in my ____, then you are _____ my _____. You will ____ the _____, and the truth will ____ you ____."

COLOR: ➡

You will know the truth, and the truth will make you free.

WRITE IT ➡

WRITE IT ➡

John 10:9

READ IT: ➡

"I am the door. If anyone enters in by me, he will be saved, and will go in and go out, and will find pasture."

FILL IN THE BLANKS: ➡

"I am the _____. If anyone _____ in by me, he will be _____, and will go __ and go ___, and will find _____."

COLOR: ➡

I am the door. If anyone enters in by me, he will be saved.

WRITE IT ➡

John 10:14-15

READ IT: ➡

"I am the good shepherd. I know my own, and I'm known by my own; even as the Father knows me, and I know the Father. I lay down my life for the

FILL IN THE BLANKS: ➡ sheep."

"I am the _____ shepherd. I _____ my own, and I'm _____ by my own; even as the _____ knows me, and I _____ the Father. I ___ down my _____ for the

COLOR: ➡ _____."

I am the good shepherd.

WRITE IT ➡

WRITE IT ➡

John 10:27-28

READ IT: ➡

"My sheep hear my voice, and I know them, and they follow me. I give eternal life to them."

FILL IN THE BLANKS: ➡

"My _____ hear my _____, and I ____ them, and they _____ me. I give _____ life to them."

COLOR: ➡

My sheep hear my voice.

WRITE IT ➡

John 11:25-26

READ IT: ➡

"I am the resurrection and the life. He who believes in me will still live, even if he dies. Whoever lives and believes in me will never die."

FILL IN THE ➡
BLANKS:

"I am the _____ and the ____. He who _____ in me will still ____, even if he ____. Whoever _____ and believes in me will _____ die."

COLOR: ➡

I am the
resurrection
and the life.

WRITE IT ➡

John 12:25-26

READ IT: ➡

"He who loves his life will lose it. He who hates his life in this world will keep it to eternal life. If anyone serves me, let him follow me."

FILL IN THE BLANKS: ➡

"He who _____ his ____ will lose it. He who _____ his life in this _____ will keep it to _____ life. If _____ serves me, let him _____ me."

COLOR: ➡

If anyone serves me, Let him follow me.

WRITE IT →

Bonus!
Free Activity Pages

TURN THE PAGE FOR *FREE* MEMORY PAGE SAMPLES
FROM THE OTHER BOOKS IN THIS SERIES!

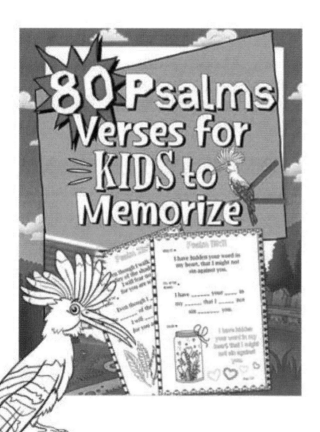

SCAN THE QR CODE TO SEE THE FULL LINEUP
OF BIBLE MEMORY BOOKS FOR KIDS!

https://www.amazon.com/dp/B0C42W4XZ9

Proverbs 16:1

READ IT: ➡

The plans of the heart
belong to man,
but the answer of the tongue
is from Yahweh.

FILL IN THE
BLANKS: ➡

The _____ of the _____
belong to ___,
but the _____ of the _____
is from _____.

COLOR: ➡

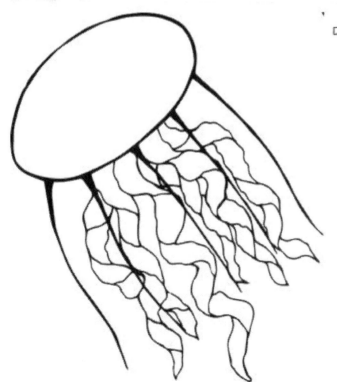

The plans of the
heart belong to
man, but the
answer of the
tongue is from
Yahweh.

HIDE THE PROVERBS IN YOUR HEART WITH 53 PROVERBS FOR KIDS TO MEMORIZE! FILL-IN-THE-BLANK VERSES, COLORING IMAGES AND BLANK LINES INCLUDED TO WRITE EVERY PROVERB FROM MEMORY. SCAN THE QR CODE TO BE TAKEN DIRECTLY TO THE AMAZON LISTING!

ISBN: 979-8393272463

Psalm 119:11

READ IT: ➡

I have hidden your word in
my heart, that I might not
sin against you.

FILL IN THE BLANKS: ➡

I have _____ your ____ in
my _____, that I _____ not
sin _____ you.

COLOR: ➡

I have hidden
your word in my
heart, that I might
not sin against
you.

MEMORIZE GOD'S TRUTH IN THE PSALMS WITH 80 PSALMS VERSES FOR KIDS TO MEMORIZE! FILL-IN-THE-BLANK VERSES, COLORING IMAGES AND BLANK LINES INCLUDED TO WRITE EVERY PROVERB FROM MEMORY. SCAN THE QR CODE TO BE TAKEN DIRECTLY TO THE AMAZON LISTING!

ISBN: 979-8843815738

Made in the USA
Columbia, SC
31 December 2024

50950745R00076